THE RESURRECTION OF JESUS OF NAZARETH

RICK JORY

WestBow Press books may be ordered through booksellers or by contacting:

WestBow Press
A Division of Thomas Nelson & Zondervan
1663 Liberty Drive
Bloomington, IN 47403
www.westbowpress.com
844-714-3454

ISBN: 979-8-3850-0073-9 (sc)
ISBN: 979-8-3850-0074-6 (hc)
ISBN: 979-8-3850-0075-3 (e)

Library of Congress Control Number: 2023911241

Print information available on the last page.

WestBow Press rev. date: 7/21/2023

WESTBOW
PRESS®
A DIVISION OF THOMAS NELSON
& ZONDERVAN

To my teaching partner in Vietnam

An Nguyen

Soli Deo Gloria

PREFACE

The greatest event in the history of humankind was not the birth of a man who claimed to be God. It was his resurrection after death.

If this truly occurred, this validated his claim.

And if the resurrection did happen, this man, Jesus of Nazareth, is truly God the Son and we must take his words seriously.

- Jesus said, "I and the Father are one" (John 10:30). Here in the Greek, the word for "one" is not in the masculine form but in the neuter. This man was not asserting that he and the Father are the same person. He is saying that he and the Father are of the same essence; that they are one in nature.

- Jesus said, "I am the resurrection and the life. Whoever believes in Me will live" (John 11:25).

- Jesus said, "I am the way and the truth and the life. No one comes to the Father except through Me" (John 14:6).

When asked what God requires of us, Jesus responded, "The work of God is this: to believe in the One He has sent" (John 6:29). Jesus clearly taught that our eternal destiny depends upon how we view him.[1] And today over 2.2 billion people throughout all parts of the world place their faith in this man, what he taught, who he is, and what his life, death, and resurrection mean.

But all of this hinges on the resurrection.

---

[1] Throughout this book, I capitalize pronouns and possessive pronouns that refer to God the Father. Those referring to Jesus are not capitalized.

Did the resurrection of Jesus of Nazareth occur?

We will look at the evidence. We will begin by discussing the Christian worldview, which is based upon the God of the Bible who has revealed Himself to His creation.

We'll then briefly describe what the Bible is.

This will be followed by a brief review of what the Bible teaches about the resurrection. This will include looking at the Hebrew Scriptures—the Christian Old Testament—as well as what Jesus said concerning his death and resurrection.

But can the Bible be trusted?

We'll look at this as well.

While our review of the resurrection will use the Bible for some of our information, we will also look at materials from sources outside the Bible, including those hostile to Christianity. We'll answer questions such as:

- Did Jesus really die on the cross?
- Was the tomb of Jesus really empty?
- Did Jesus truly rise from the dead?
- What exactly does the resurrection imply? What does it mean?

If the resurrection of Jesus truly happened, this changes everything.

CONTENTS

1. THE CHRISTIAN WORLDVIEW

A worldview is a philosophy of life. It is a person's conception of the world and how they view and interpret the things around them. A worldview can be defined by how one answers the following, although worldviews can encompass far more than this:

Origin: Where did we come from?
Identity: Who are we?
Meaning: Why are we here?
Morality: How should we live?
Destiny: What happens when we die?

If there is no God, no supernatural ("outside of nature") Creator, we are left with formulating answers along the lines of the following.

Origin: Where did we come from?

Without a Creator, without purposeful design, all of this "just happened." Over billions and billions of years, atoms assembled into more and more complex compounds, which became the cosmos. Some of these eventually (magically) came to life. Over time lifeforms evolved in their complexity and sophistication, ultimately leading to a class of animals we call "humans." We are a mix of chemicals—readily available substances worth about a dollar.[2]

Identity: Who are we?

We are a cosmic fluke, a cosmic accident. We are not here by design or purpose.

Meaning: Why are we here?

There is no real meaning to life. Things randomnly happened.

Morality: How should we live?

There is no overriding authority establishing the requirements or standards as to how we are to live. There is no moral law and no reason to live in any certain way. Each person can determine for themselves what is right, what is wrong, and how they want to live.

Destiny: What happens when we die?

Since only the material exists, there is no immaterial part of who we are. Our "conscience" is imaginary. There is no such thing as the human "soul." When we die, we cease to exist.

---

[2] See Anne Marie Helmenstine, Ph.D., "How much are the elements in your body worth?" published in *ThoughtCo*, January 13, 2020 and available at https://www.thoughtco.com/worth-of-your-elements-3976054 (accessed November 23, 2021).

The Christian worldview recognizes a God of creation. And we believe God has revealed Himself to this creation. We base our worldview on what God has revealed—recognizing He has revealed Himself in a number of ways:

- God is revealed through the creation itself. The Psalmist writes,

> The heavens declare the glory of God,
>
> the skies proclaim the work of His hands.
>
> Day after day they pour forth speech,
>
> night after night they reveal knowledge.
>
> Without speech or language,
>
> without a sound to be heard,
>
> their voice has gone out into all the earth,
>
> their words to the ends of the world (Psalm 19:1–4).

In talking about the godless, those who refuse to acknowledge God or give Him glory, the Apostle Paul writes, "What may be known about God is plain to them, because God has made it plain to them. For since the creation of the world God's invisible qualities, His eternal power and divine nature, have been clearly seen, being understood from His workmanship, so that men are without excuse" (Romans 1:19–20).

- God has revealed Himself through history.

The fact that there is a group of people scattered all throughout the world recognized as Jews testifies to the acts of God. The Jews did not choose God. They came about because of God's promise to a Gentile: Abraham. It was through Abraham's descendants that God would reveal Himself. These chosen people of God, descendants of Abraham and the "children of the promise," were subsequently called Jews—the Jewish identity coming about through an act of God.

Think about this—this promise to Abraham. We find its first mention in the twelfth chapter of the first book of the Bible, that is, Genesis 12. Abraham is told that he would be the father of many nations. Both the Arabs and the Jews trace their ancestry to this single individual—a migrant from Mesopotamia.

What made this one man in this remote part of the world so special? He had no army. He ruled no great nation. We have nothing that he wrote down—nor do we know if he could even write. We know very little about his history until he was chosen by God to change the world.

He was told he would do this through his descendants despite this promise coming when Abraham was in his seventies and his elderly wife was barren. Abraham was childless until he had his son Ishmael through his wife's maid Hagar. At the time Abraham was seventy-six. His descendants through Hagar become the Arab nations, today comprising four hundred fifty million people.

It wasn't until Abraham was one hundred that he has his son Isaac through his wife Sarah. His descendants through Isaac and Isaac's son Jacob are the Jews, numbering fifteen million people.

And Christians are spiritual descendants of Abraham through faith. These number 2.2 billion!

Arabs and Jews have maintained an identity throughout thousands of years. I don't know any Macedonians or Romans or Canaanites or Edomites, but I do know several Arabs and several Jews. This is a witness to just one of God's many acts in history.

- God has revealed Himself through His spokesmen.

Prophets brought the words of God to the people including describing in detail events before they occurred. Fulfilled prophecy authenticates the prophetic word and its true author. Only God, who is outside the dimension of time, can account for this.

- God has revealed Himself through His word.

Prophets and others called by God wrote down God's words, which became Judaism's Scripture (the Hebrew Scriptures) and the Christian Old Testament. To this was added the New Testament—written to describe this man, Jesus of Nazareth, and words from those who saw him. We will look in more detail at what the Bible is, and whether we can trust what it says.

- God has revealed Himself through His word becoming flesh.

The birth, death, and resurrection of Jesus of Nazareth represents God appearing on Earth in human form. The Bible explains from its opening pages why God did this. The earliest mention of Jesus' mission is found in the third chapter of the Bible's first book—the fifteenth verse (Genesis 3:15).

- God has revealed Himself through transformed lives.

Throughout human history, we have seen lives transformed by the presence of God in the form of the Holy Spirit.

The Christian worldview encompasses God's revealed truth and is based on His revealed truths. Because of this, the Christian worldview offers completely different answers from what we saw above. Here is a brief overview of the Christian worldview.

The Christian World View—Origin: Where did we come from?

I like to phrase this question differently: To whom or to what do we owe our existence?

We believe the universe was created. It did not come about on its own. The Bible teaches that in the beginning God created the heavens and the earth. We believe the creation itself bears witness to its Creator.

The universe, and life itself was purposefully created. The ordered, rational universe—one that operates on laws and principles and is finely tuned for life to exist—suggests creation was not blind or accidental. All that we see is here on purpose, precisely designed with foresight and planning.

The Christian World View—Identity: Who are we?

All humans were created in the image of God, who has a plan and a purpose for each one of us. As image bearers of God, each one of us is unique, has special value, and is here purposefully.

The Christian World View—Meaning: Why are we here?

We are here to glorify God. We are His. Jesus tells us there are two possible paths to take through life—the way of the thief, who robs one's life, kills one's life, and destroys one's life—or his way, where we achieve the life God wants us to have (John 10:10).

The Christian World View—Morality: How should we live?

Morality comes from the Moral Lawgiver—God. Jesus also said there are only two commandments: love God and love others (Mark 12:30–21). We are to live in such a way that we bring glory to our Creator. We do this by loving Him, and loving all participants in God's creation.

The Christian World View—Destiny: Where are we going?

The Christian worldview listens to the voice of the One who said, "I go and prepare a place for you. And if I go and prepare a place for you, I will come back and welcome you into My presence, so that you also may be where I am" (John 14:3). Our destiny is the eventual new earth where there is no disease, no death, no mourning, and no sin. It is what the God of Creation intended for this earth until our rebellion against God marred us as image bearers and led to the earth's bondage to death and decay.

We also believe in the immaterial part of who we are—our soul. Souls do not die. This is true for "believers" as well as for "non-believers." All will live through eternity. But unless called into the kingdom of God, one's fate will be one of a godless existence. God never forces anyone to be with Him.

Since much of our worldview centers on God's written word, we'll now briefly describe this—what Christians call the "Bible."

2. THE BIBLE

The Bible is a collection of materials from some forty different authors written over a period of roughly fifteen hundred years. These writings were developed long before the advent of the printing press. Transmission of the text was through manual copying. Because of the sacred nature of the text, copies were made under the strictest of rules and care, with copies carefully preserved for future generations. This is why we have been able to retrieve more from this group of writings than from any other writings from antiquity.

The Bible consists of two main sections. The first part comes to us from ancient Hebrew sacred writings—the Hebrew Scriptures. Christianity labels these the "Old Testament" (old covenant). The discovery of the Dead Sea Scrolls, which began in 1947, helps prove the accuracy of the transmission of the text of the Old Testament. Writings dated around 150 to 100 B.C. (one hundred to one hundred fifty years before the birth of Jesus of Nazareth) were part of this discovery. Scholars have poured over these findings. They recognize that the text of these ancient writings are almost exactly the same as writings that are dated 800 A.D. (eight hundred years after Jesus). Despite repeated manual copying done over a period of nine hundred to nine hundred fifty years, the later texts match the earliest texts. Copying (transmission) has been virtually without error.

Perhaps the most impressive example of this is something referred to as "The Great Isaiah Scroll." These are the writings of the Jewish prophet Isaiah found as part of the Dead Sea discovery. The text from this scroll, written at least one hundred years before Jesus ever walked on the earth, is virtually identical to what we find in today's Hebrew Scriptures (our Old Testament).[3]

The second major section of the Bible is referred to as the "New Testament." It covers the period when Jesus walked on the earth and immediately afterwards. The transmission accuracy of the New Testament can be evidenced by the thousands of copies of the ancient manuscripts (MSS), or portions of these writings, that have been discovered, and the minimal variations seen between these writings. These copies of the MSS were found in different geographical locations and are dated at different time periods. Yet, there are minimal variations among them.

Throughout the ages, there were scribes who meticulously copied the Bible from generation to generation. We see the accuracy and long-term reliability of the text as is clear from archeology and the manuscript evidence. Later we'll look with more detail as to whether we can trust the Bible. We know the transmission of the text was accurate. But are the words themselves trustworthy?

We'll do this after we look at a portion of what the Bible says about the resurrection of Jesus.

---

[3] The finding of the Great Isaiah Scroll marks as one of the greatest archeological discoveries of the last century. This specific text is important for at least three reasons. It shows the phenomenal accuracy of the transmission of the text—over close to a one-thousand-year period. Secondly, Isaiah describes the Messiah in detail, including details of the crucifixion. The Great Isaiah Scroll proves that the text was not altered after the fact—changed so as to reflect what Jesus of Nazareth experienced (we'll discuss this). Lastly, at one time there was a school of thought that Isaiah 1-39 and Isaiah 40-66 were written by two different authors. We do not see this break in the Great Isaiah Scroll—chapter 39 and chapter 40 are connected in the same column on this scroll.

3. Predictions of the Resurrection – From the Hebrew Scriptures

Jesus told the religious leaders of his day, "You pore over the Scriptures because you presume that by them you possess eternal life. These are the very words that testify about Me" (John 5:39). The book *A Forty-Day Study of the Biblical Story: The Story of Christ, Volume One* goes through the Old Testament showing how it points to Jesus of Nazareth.[4]

We find considerable information in the Hebrew Scriptures concerning Jesus. Our first glimpse of his mission and his suffering comes from the earliest pages of the Bible. Satan, appearing as a serpent, approaches Eve in the garden of Eden and tells her not to trust God's word. Both Adam and Eve go against God's command, whereupon God confronts Satan and tells him,

> "I will put enmity between you and the woman,
>
> and between your seed and her seed.
>
> He will crush your head,
>
> and you will strike his heel." (Genesis 3:15)

---

[4] Rick Jory, *A Forty-Day Study of the Biblical Story – The Story of Christ, Volume One: Preparing the Way* (Bloomington, WestBow Press, 2020).

A Deliverer, the seed of woman, will crush Satan. But in return, Satan "will strike his heel." A serpent strike is deadly. This Deliverer will defeat Satan, but in the process he will be afflicted and will suffer death.

God reveals this Deliverer progressively, over time, and we are told many things about him throughout the Old Testament. He is referred to as the Messiah—God's Anointed. The New Testament reveals that this Deliverer is Jesus of Nazareth.

As mentioned, Christians base their worldview on the Bible—including that there is life after death. The Hebrew Scriptures talk of this certainty. As one example, Israel's king David committed adultery with Bathsheba and his child from this union dies (2 Samuel 12). While this son is ill, David mourns. But once the child dies, David stops his mourning and worships God.

David's behavior confuses those around him. When asked to explain this, David responds, "While the child was alive, I fasted and wept, for I said, 'Who knows? The LORD may be gracious to me and let him live.' But now that he is dead, why should I fast? Can I bring him back again? *I will go to him, but he will not return to me*" (2 Samuel 12:22–23; emphasis added). David foresees a time when he and the dead child will be united—and this will be in the afterlife.

The Hebrew Scriptures clearly foresee a general bodily resurrection of Jews whose names are written in the book of life:

> At that time Michael, the great prince who stands watch over your people, will rise up. There will be a time of distress, the likes of which will not have occurred from the beginning of nations until that time. But at that time your people—everyone whose name is found written in the book—will be delivered.

> And many who sleep in the dust of the earth will awake, some to everlasting life, but others to shame and everlasting contempt. Then the wise will shine like the brightness of the heavens, and those who lead many to righteousness will shine like the stars forever and ever. (Daniel 12:1–3)

This does not relate to the New Testament teaching concerning the rapture of the Church. The text applies to "your people" (Israel) and the events occur after the tribulation ("a time of distress"). The text implies a resurrection of the Messiah—for several reasons. It is the Messiah who delivers the people of Israel (we find this from other text of the Hebrew Scriptures) and it is the Messiah who leads the people of Israel "to righteousness."

The Psalmist writes, "But God will redeem my life from Sheol, for He will surely take me to Himself" (Psalm 49:15, "Sheol" is the grave, the place of the dead).

Isaiah writes that death will be swallowed up forever (Isaiah 25:8) and tells us,

> Our dead will live; their bodies will rise.
>
> Awake and sing, you who dwell in the dust!
>
> For your dew is like the dew of the morning,
>
> and the earth will bring forth her dead. (Isaiah 26:19).

Through the prophet Hosea, God tells us:

> I will ransom them from the power of Sheol;
>
> I will redeem them from Death.
>
> Where, O Death, are your plagues?
>
> Where, O Sheol, is your sting? (Hosea 13:14)

A portion of this is quoted by the Apostle Paul in 1 Corinthians 15:55.

These texts are referencing "life after death," not resurrection as depicted by the events surrounding Jesus. Are their places in the Hebrew Scriptures that truly relate to the resurrection Jesus experienced?

Yes.

We find these words in the book of Job:

> But I know that my Redeemer lives,
>
> and in the end He will stand upon the earth.
>
> Even after my skin has been destroyed,
>
> yet in my flesh I will see God.
>
> I will see Him for myself,
>
> my eyes will behold Him, and not as a stranger.
>
> How my heart yearns within me! (Job 19:25–27)

These words reflect an afterlife ("…yet in my flesh I will see God") and also the resurrection of the Messiah ("…my Redeemer lives!").

When Jesus was on the cross, he uttered the words, "My God, my God, why have You forsaken me?" This is recorded in the New Testament by both Matthew and Mark (Matthew 27:46; Mark 15:34). Jesus is quoting from Psalm 22—a "Messianic Psalm" that clearly depicts the crucifixion. While the Psalm begins with a description of pain, suffering, and rejection, it ends with resurrection:

> I will proclaim Your name to my brothers,
>
> I will praise You in the assembly.
>
> You who fear the LORD, praise Him!
>
> All descendants of Jacob, honor Him!
>
> All offspring of Israel, revere Him!
>
> For He has not despised or detested
>
> the torment of the afflicted.
>
> He has not hidden His face from him,
>
> but has attended to his cry for help. (Psalm 22:22–24)

In another Messianic Psalm, we see the words: "For You will not abandon my soul to Sheol, nor will You let Your Holy One see decay" (Psalm 16:10—"Holy One" is a reference to the Messiah, Jesus).

Many of the verses from the prophet Isaiah discuss the Messiah. Isaiah 53 describes the crucifixion in detail—despite having been written seven hundred years before the event, and it also foresees the resurrection:

Yet it was the LORD's will to crush Him

and to cause Him to suffer

and when His soul is made a guilt offering,

He will see His offspring, He will prolong His days,

and the good pleasure of the LORD will prosper in His hand.

After the anguish of His soul,

He will see the light of life and be satisfied.

By His knowledge My righteous Servant will justify many,

and He will bear their iniquities. (Isaiah 53:10–11)

The Hebrew Scriptures contain an interesting story Jesus uses to relate to his resurrection. This comes to us in the events associated with the prophet Jonah. His story is well known.

Told by God to travel to Nineveh and warn the godless Ninevites of their impending doom unless they repent, Jonah refused. He objected to doing anything which would benefit Nineveh, Israel's enemy. He books passage on a ship headed in the opposite direction from Nineveh only to have the ship experience a violent storm. Jonah is blamed for this and is thrown overboard. He is swallowed by a great fish but delivered after three days.

Jesus uses this to describe his death—and his resurrection that will occur three days later. We'll get to this.

We also get a hint at three days and then resurrection from the words of the prophet Hosea:

Come, let us return to the LORD.

For He has torn us to pieces,

but He will heal us

He has wounded us,

but He will bind up our wounds.

After two days He will revive us

on the third day He will raise us up,

that we may live in His presence. (Hosea 6:1–2)

The clearest predictions concerning resurrection come from Jesus, himself. We'll now look at this.

4. Predictions of the Resurrection – From Jesus

Throughout the New Testament there are hints of Jesus' sacrificial death. The first comes even before Jesus was born. The Bible tells us that a heavenly host of angels were present at the birth of Jesus. The angels appear to shepherds in their fields.

We are also told that Mary, the mother of Jesus, wrapped the baby Jesus in "swaddling cloths." He was also placed in a manger—a trough used to feed animals.

All of this is unusual, until we piece together what is implied. The Greek term for swaddling cloths is found in only two places in the Bible. Luke 2:7 says:

> And she gave birth to her firstborn son and wrapped him in swaddling cloths and
> laid him in a manger, because there was no place for them in the inn. (ESV)

And in a few verses later, Luke 2:12 tells us that angels appeared to shepherds, telling them that the Messiah has come and what to look for:

> "And this will be the sign: you will find a baby wrapped in swaddling cloths and lying in a manger."

So, the sign these shepherds were to look for was not just any baby, but a baby wrapped in swaddling cloths and a baby placed in a feeding trough.

What on earth is being implied here?

Because of the location of these shepherds and their fields—just three miles from the Jerusalem temple—historians suggest that these were "priestly shepherds." These were men who could only begin their work at age thirty, similar to the Levitical priests in the temple. Their jobs were to raise and care for the animals that would be used in the temple sacrifices for the atonement of the people's sins. The animals had to be unblemished. They could not have torn skin or broken legs.[5]

To protect a newborn lamb, the shepherds would take the lamb, wrap it in cloth strips—swaddling cloths—and place it in a feeding trough so that it could not try to run and possibly damage its fragile body.

The act of wrapping the baby Jesus in swaddling cloths, and placing it in a feeding trough, wasn't an accident. This was God's grand orchestration, telling the shepherds, and you and me, that this child laying in a manger would be the Lamb of God that would atone for the people's sins.

This baby had come to die. And when Jesus began his ministry, John the Baptist referred to him as the "Lamb of God that takes away the sins of the world" (John 1:29).

But there is far more that point to Jesus' sacrificial death. After his first miracle, Jesus goes to Jerusalem and appears in the temple. He tells those present, "Destroy this temple, and in three days I will raise it up again" (John 2:19). These words are taken literally by those who scoff at him. "This temple took forty-six years to build, and You are going to raise it up in three days?" (John 2:20). But John, in describing this event in his Gospel, adds clarity:

---

[5] As stated, the God of Christianity has not remained distanced from His creation. Part of His instruction to His chosen people involved the temple and temple sacrifices. The book of Leviticus in twenty-four separate places discuss animals for sacrifice having to be unblemished.

But Jesus was speaking about the temple of His body. After He was raised from the dead, His disciples remembered that He had said this. Then they believed the Scripture and the word that Jesus had spoken. (John 2:21–22).

Here Jesus hints both of his death—and as importantly, of his resurrection that would occur three days after his death.

After this event in the temple, we are told of an encounter between Jesus and a religious leader of Judea, Nicodemus. Jesus refers to him as "*the* teacher of Israel" (John 3:10, ESV). Jesus tells him, "Truly, truly, I tell you, no one can see the kingdom of God unless he is born again" and explains the necessity of regeneration through the Holy Spirit for one to experience eternity with God. Jesus mentions his death:

"Just as Moses lifted up the snake in the wilderness, so the Son of Man must be lifted up, that everyone who believes in Him may have eternal life.

For God so loved the world that He gave His one and only Son, that everyone who believes in Him shall not perish but have eternal life." (John 3:14–16)

Here, he is reminding *the* teacher of Israel of an incident that happened when God's chosen people had left Egypt and were en route to the land God had promised them. His reference to being "lifted up" foreshadows the cross.

As to the incident, God had delivered the people of Israel from Egyptian bondage but they continually complained and showed their lack of trust in God. God sends venomous snakes among the people as punishment for their sin—but He also provides for their deliverance. Moses is told, "Make a fiery serpent and mount it on a pole. When anyone who is bitten looks at it, he will live" (Numbers 21:8).

Jesus tells Nicodemus, "Just as Moses lifted up the snake in the wilderness, so the Son of Man must be lifted up, that everyone who believes in Him may have eternal life." Jesus is referencing his death but also the deliverance he provides. Those who place their faith in him are given eternal life.

Here we also see the term, "Son of Man." This was Jesus' self-reference. It comes from a vision recorded by the prophet Daniel found in the Hebrew Scriptures:

> In my vision in the night I continued to watch,
> and I saw One like the Son of Man
> coming with the clouds of heaven.
> He approached the Ancient of Days
> and was led into His presence.
> And He was given dominion,
> glory, and kingship,
> that the people of every nation and language
> should serve Him.
> His dominion is an everlasting dominion
> that will not pass away,
> and His kingdom is one
> that will never be destroyed. (Daniel 7:13–14)

The "Ancient of Days" is God the Father. According to Daniel's vision, this "Son of Man" has been in the presence of God and will be given rule over the entire earth. In this same convesation with Nicodemus, Jesus tells him, "No one has ever gone into heaven except the one who came from heaven—the Son of Man" (John 3:13, NIV). That Jesus will be given a kingdom that will be everlasting and will never be destroyed suggests resurrection from his death.

Toward the end of his earthly ministry, Jesus did not keep his impending death a secret from his disciples. He was also clear that he would be resurrected, although his disciples did not readily understand what Jesus was telling them. There is an important event described by Matthew, Mark, and Luke where Jesus travels to Caesarea Philippi—a place known for pagan worship.

Matthew provides the most complete description of what happened. Jesus asks his disciples, "Who do people say the Son of Man is?" Here we see the term "Son of Man" once again. Matthew tells us:

They replied, "Some say John the Baptist; others say Elijah; and still others, Jeremiah or one of the prophets."

"But what about you?" Jesus asked. "Who do you say I am?"

Simon Peter answered, "You are the Christ, the Son of the living God."

Jesus replied, "Blessed are you, Simon son of Jonah! For this was not revealed to you by flesh and blood, but by My Father in heaven. And I tell you that you are Peter, and on this rock I will build My church, and the gates of Hades will not prevail against it. (Matthew 16:14–18).

Immediately after this event, Matthew adds, "From that time on Jesus began to show His disciples that He must go to Jerusalem and suffer many things at the hands of the elders, chief priests, and scribes, and that *He must be killed and on the third day be raised to life*" (Matthew 16:21; emphasis added).

Matthew, Mark, and Luke record a second time when Jesus predicted his death and resurrection. Matthew writes: When they gathered together in Galilee, Jesus told them, 'The Son of Man is about to be delivered into the hands of men. *They will kill Him, and on the third day He will be raised to life.*' And the disciples were deeply grieved (Matthew 17:22–23; emphasis added—note again Jesus' self-reference as "Son of Man").

John records another event where Jesus speaks of his death:

Six days before the Passover, Jesus came to Bethany, the hometown of Lazarus, whom He had raised from the dead. So they hosted a dinner for Jesus there. Martha served, and Lazarus was among those reclining at the table with Him. Then Mary took about a pint of expensive perfume, made of pure nard, and she anointed Jesus' feet and wiped them with her hair. And the house was filled with the fragrance of the perfume.

But one of His disciples, Judas Iscariot, who was going to betray Him, asked, "Why wasn't this perfume sold for three hundred denarii and the money given to the poor?" Judas did not say this because he cared about the poor, but because he was a thief. As keeper of the money bag, he used to take from what was put into it.

"Leave her alone," Jesus replied. "She has kept this perfume in preparation for the day of My burial. The poor you will always have with you, *but you will not always have Me.*" (John 12:1–8; emphasis added)

Jesus will proceed to Jerusalem to observe the Passover—and to allow for his arrest and crucifixion. Once again, he tells his disciples what is about to happen:

As Jesus was going up to Jerusalem, He took the twelve disciples aside and said, "Look, we are going up to Jerusalem, and the Son of Man will be delivered over to the chief priests and scribes. They will condemn Him to death and will deliver Him over to the Gentiles *to be mocked and flogged and crucified. And on the third day He will be raised to life.*" (Matthew 20:17–19; emphasis added)

At the Passover supper, his last meal with the disciples before the crucifixion, he announces he will be going away—but will return. From John 14 through 17, we clearly see Jesus knowing ahead of time of his crucifixion as well as his resurrection and ascension to the Father.

5. THE SIGN OF JONAH

In the preceding section, we showed how Jesus was aware of his impending death as well as his resurrection that would occur three days later. While he spoke of this to his disciples, he also announced this to the religious leaders—his adversaries.

Matthew describes this event in detail. Jesus heals a demon-possessed man who is both blind and mute (Matthew 12:22). The people witnessing this event are astonished and begin to see Jesus as the Messiah—the Son of David (Matthew 12:23). But the most religious people in Jesus' day, the scribes and Pharisees, claim that Jesus is performing his miracles through the power of Satan. They demand another miracle (sign).

From Matthew:

Jesus replied, "A wicked and adulterous generation demands a sign, but none will be given it except the sign of the prophet Jonah. For as Jonah was three days and three nights in the belly of the great fish, so the Son of Man will be three days and three nights in the heart of the earth" (Matthew 12:39–40).

Jesus had done enough, and has had enough. He knew that the Pharisees and the religious leadership of Judaism would remain spiritually blind. They have rejected their Messiah and Son of God. He tells them he will no longer do miracles to authenticate who he is—except one. Jesus calls this the "sign of the prophet Jonah"—and it centers on resurrection. "For as Jonah was three days and three nights in the belly of the great fish, so the Son of Man will be three days and three nights in the heart of the earth." Jesus will die and be three days and nights in the grave. Jonah survives the three days in the giant fish. Jesus will be resurrected after three days in the grave. This sign is intended for the Jews. It is to be the final sign authenticating Jesus as Messiah and Son of God. The sign of Jonah will be shown to the Jewish people on three occasions. Two of these have occurred. The third and final sign of Jonah will occur in the future.

We'll briefly look at these.

6. A Sign of Jonah: The Resurrection of Lazarus

The first sign of Jonah occurs just two miles from Jerusalem and just a short time before Jesus' own death. Jesus had become close friends with Mary, her sister Martha, and their brother, Lazarus, who live in Bethany. In John 11, we are told that Lazarus had fallen ill, so Mary and Martha send word to Jesus, "Lord, the one You love is sick" (John 11:3).

Jesus knows that Lazarus has died, and he purposefully delays returning to Bethany until Lazarus has been in the tomb four days (John 11:17). The sign of Jonah is to convince the Jews of who Jesus is. We're told that, due to Bethany's close proximity to Jerusalem, many Jews came to console Mary and Martha on the loss of their brother (John 11:18–19).

Jesus tells Martha, "Your brother will rise again" and announces, "I am the resurrection and the life. Whoever believes in Me will live, even though he dies. And everyone who lives and believes in Me will never die" (John 11:23, 25–26).

He orchestrates the raising of Lazarus for the glory of God (John 11:40). Again, he is doing this as a sign.

John tells us,

Then Jesus lifted His eyes upward and said, "Father, I thank You that You have heard Me. I knew that You always hear Me, but I say this *for the benefit of the people standing here, so they may believe that You sent Me.*"

After Jesus had said this, He called out in a loud voice, "Lazarus, come out!" (John 11:41–43; emphasis added).

Jesus is doing this so that those present may believe in who he is. And when he calls Lazarus to come out of the tomb, it is in a loud voice. I interpret this not relating to Lazarus being hard of hearing, but to make sure the Jews nearby understood it is the actions of Jesus that bring Lazarus forth from the grave.

This first sign of Jonah had the desired effect. John tells us, "Therefore many of the Jews who had come to Mary, and had seen what Jesus did, believed in Him" (John 11:45). Many, though, rejected Jesus and this sign and we are told that, "… from that day on they plotted to kill Him" (John 11:53).

Six days before the Passover—the week of the crucifixion—Jesus returns to Bethany. We're told:

Meanwhile a large crowd of Jews learned that Jesus was there. And they came not only because of Him, but also to see Lazarus, whom He had raised from the dead. So the chief priests made plans to kill Lazarus as well, for on account of him many of the Jews were deserting them and believing in Jesus. (John 12:9–11)

The story of the raising of Lazarus is important, but it is only found in John's Gospel. It is omitted from the Gospels written by Matthew, Mark, and Luke.

Why?

Though speculation, it is not hard to come up with a possible reason. Lazarus was what we would call a "marked man." The Jewish religious leadership wants to kill him. Matthew, Mark, and Luke all wrote their accounts of Jesus much earlier than John's writing. It is possible that when they wrote their Gospels, Lazarus was still alive and they did not want to draw attention to him because of the events at Bethany. By the time John wrote his Gospel, it is possible that Lazarus had died and there were no risks to Lazarus by John sharing this story.

The raising of Lazarus created quite a stir. The next day Jesus enters Jerusalem for Passover week, and John tells us:

The next day the great crowd that had come to the feast heard that Jesus was coming to Jerusalem. They took palm branches and went out to meet Him, shouting:

"Hosanna!"

"Blessed is He who comes in the name of the Lord!"

"Blessed is the King of Israel!" (John 12:12–13)

John adds these important words:

Meanwhile, many people continued to testify that *they had been with Jesus when He called Lazarus from the tomb and raised him from the dead. That is also why the crowd went out to meet Him, because they heard that He had performed this sign.*

Then the Pharisees said to one another, "You can see that this is doing you no good. Look how the whole world has gone after Him!" (John 12:17–19; emphasis added)

Before we leave this first "sign of Jonah," we see, once again, Jesus' prediction of his death and also his resurrection:

Now My soul is troubled, and what shall I say? 'Father, save Me from this hour'? No, it is for this purpose that I have come to this hour. Father, glorify Your name!"

Then a voice came from heaven: "I have glorified it, and I will glorify it again."

The crowd standing there heard it and said that it had thundered. Others said that an angel had spoken to Him.

In response, Jesus said, "This voice was not for My benefit, but yours. Now judgment is upon this world; now the prince of this world will be cast out. And I, when I am lifted up from the earth, will draw everyone to Myself." He said this to indicate the kind of death He was going to die.

The crowd replied, "We have heard from the Law that the Christ will remain forever. So how can you say that the Son of Man must be lifted up? Who is this Son of Man?"

Then Jesus told them, "For a little while longer, the Light will be among you. Walk while you have the Light, so that darkness will not overtake you. The one who walks in the darkness does not know where he is going. While you have the Light, believe in the Light, so that you may become sons of light."

After Jesus had spoken these things, He went away and was hidden from them. (John 12:27–36)

7. A Sign of Jonah: The Resurrection of the Two Witnesses

The final sign of Jonah occurs after the rapture of the Church and during the great tribulation, where the Jewish people are suffering intense persecution.[6]

Jesus promised the "sign of Jonah"—his death and resurrection. But even after his resurrection and appearance in Jerusalem, most of the Jewish people continued in spiritual blindness.

The Apostle Paul discusses this rejection in a letter her wrote to the Jesus-followers in Rome. He was distraught over the rejection of the Messiah by his Jewish brothers and sisters. He explains why this has occurred:

> I do not want you to be ignorant of this mystery, brothers, so that you will not be conceited:
> A hardening in part has come to Israel, until the full number of the Gentiles has come in.
> (Romans 11:25)

---

[6] This statement assumes the Church is raptured *before* the tribulation (a "pre-trib" position

Though Israel has rejected the Messiah, God has not abandoned Israel. But He has hardened the hearts of most of the Jews. Paul tells us this is temporary. It lasts "until the full number of the Gentiles has come in." It last until the Church contains the number of Gentiles God desires to call into His family.

What are God's future plans for Israel?

Before their deliverance from the tribulation, God sends two witnesses to the Jewish people. They appear in Jerusalem and preach to the people for 1,260 days (Revelation 11:2–3).

When the two witnesses have finished their testimony, the beast that comes up from the Abyss will wage war with them, and will overpower and kill them. Their bodies will lie in the street of the great city—figuratively called Sodom and Egypt—where their Lord was also crucified. For three and a half days all peoples and tribes and tongues and nations will view their bodies and will not permit them to be laid in a tomb. And those who dwell on the earth will gloat over them, and will celebrate and send one another gifts, because these two prophets had tormented them. (Revelation 11:7–10)

The two witnesses are killed and their bodies remain in view for three and a half days. The sign of Jonah involves resurrection. We are told:

But after the three and a half days, the breath of life from God entered the two witnesses, and they stood on their feet, and great fear fell upon those who saw them. And the witnesses heard a loud voice from heaven saying, "Come up here." And they went up to heaven in a cloud as their enemies watched them. (Revelation 11:11–12)

This is the third and final sign of Jonah. But now, more and more Jews will come to Christ. And it is at this point that Jesus will return. Paul writes,

And so all Israel will be saved, as it is written:

> "The Deliverer will come from Zion.
> He will remove godlessness from Jacob.
> And this is My covenant with them
> when I take away their sins." (Romans 11:26–27)

There will come a time in the future when the Jews will call upon the name of the Lord and they will be delivered (saved). Jesus will return as King of kings and Lord of lords. The prophet Zechariah describes this event:

> Then I will pour out on the house of David and on the people of Jerusalem a spirit of grace and prayer, and they will look on Me, the One they have pierced. They will mourn for Him as one mourns for an only child and grieve bitterly for Him as one grieves for a firstborn son. (Zechariah 12:10)

8. THE SIGN OF JONAH: THE RESURRECTION OF JESUS OF NAZARETH

The death and resurrection of Jesus of Nazareth is central to Christianity and the Gospel message. If you look at the Gospel writings, the historical accounts of Jesus while he was on the earth, one-fourth of Luke's writing is devoted to the week of Jesus' death and resurrection (Luke 19–24). A third of Matthew's writing covers this week (Matthew 21–28), as does a third of Mark's writing (Mark 11–16). A full one-half of John's Gospel is devoted to this (John 12–20).

The book of Acts describes the earliest days of the Church. It begins by describing the resurrected Jesus and his ascension. There are almost two dozen references to resurrection in the book of Acts, and we see verses like:

Acts 2:24	"But God raised him from the dead…"
Acts 2:32	"God has raised this Jesus to life…"
Acts 3:15	"…but God raised him from the dead."
Acts 4:10	"Jesus Christ of Nazareth, whom you crucified but whom God raised from the dead…"
Acts 5:30	"The God of our fathers raised Jesus from the dead…"
Acts 10:40	"…but God raised him on the third day and caused hm to be seen."
Acts 13:30	"But God raised him from the dead…"

Acts 13:34   "…God raised him from the dead…"
Acts 13:37   "…the one whom God raised from the dead…"

I could add to this list, but you get the point. The early Church centered its message on the resurrection of Jesus. And one practice of the early church continues to this day. The resurrection occured on the first day of the week, so believers in Jesus began meeting on this day in celebration of this event.

Later we'll discuss what the resurrection meant, but you'll note that up until now we've focused on information contained in the Bible. But can we trust those words? Is the Bible reliable?

That's what we'll look at next.

9. CAN THE BIBLE BE TRUSTED?

Christianity is based on facts—historical facts. This is true of the Bible as well. The Bible was written by men throughout history and Christianity's foundation rests on events in history. History lends itself to investigation.

Archeology can help determine whether events recorded in the Bible represent truth or fiction. The analysis of ancient writings outside of the Bible can collaborate historical events. Ancient writings from other geographical regions and cultures outside of the biblical story can be investigated to see if they parallel or conflict with what the Bible has to say concerning such things as important people, important locations, and important events. The accuracy, reliability, and trustworthiness of the Bible is well documented and numerous books are available that address this in considerable detail. But let's briefly look into this.

There are at least ten items that acclaim the Bible's veracity. These include:

1. The documents themselves (manuscript evidence)
2. Archaeological evidence
3. Eyewitness accounts associated with the text
4. Corroborating accounts
5. Consistency

6. Prophetic accuracy

7. Expert scrutiny

8. Leader acceptance

9. Global influence

10. Changed lives

We're going to briefly look at each of these, particularly as they relate to the biblical accounts of Jesus' death and resurrection.

1. **The documents themselves (manuscript evidence)**

There are considerably more copies of the biblical manuscripts, with remarkable consistency between them, than there are *for any of the classics like Plato, Aristotle, and Socrates.* We actually have *more writings on Jesus than we do the Roman emperor Julius Caesar.* As mentioned, the finding of the Great Isaiah Scroll in 1947 helps verify the accuracy of the biblical transmission.

We have 5,700 handwritten Greek manuscripts (MSS) of the New Testament and more than 9,000 MSS written in other languages. Some of the MSS fragments date to 50 – 70 A.D.

Separate from this, in the writings of the early church fathers we find frequent quotes from the biblical text (scholars have counted over 36,000 quotes). If we did not have any of the biblical manuscripts themselves, we could use these quoted sections *to reproduce all but eleven verses of the New Testament!*

2. **Archaeological Evidence**

William M. Ramsay (1851-1939) was curious as to the accuracy of the Bible. He set out to investigate archaeologically items found in the book of Acts, a record of the earliest days of the Christian movement. Acts was written by Luke, a travelling companion of the Apostle Paul.

The more Ramsay traveled throughout the regions described by Luke, the more he saw the astonishing accuracy of Luke's writing. Geographical names, locations and boundaries, titles of officials, names of individuals, the various dates when events were said to have occurred—all were found to be accurate. Ramsay concluded that Luke should be ranked among the greatest of historians. Other researchers have come to the same conclusion. Scores of the details contained in Luke's writings have been authenticated archeologically and by sources outside the Bible (this is true for other biblical writings as well).

For what it's worth, based on the success of Ramsay's work, a second researcher conducted the same type of archeological/historical research looking at the writings of the Apostle John. Fifty-nine facts from John's Gospel have been verified. Much of what John records in his Gospel takes place in and around Jerusalem—but Jerusalem was totally destroyed in 70 A.D. It is only relatively recently that archeologists have uncovered such biblical sites as the Pool of Siloam and the Pool of Bethesda (both described by John with his descriptions matching the archeological findings).

Thirty-nine of the people mentioned in the New Testament have been confirmed as historical by archaeology and *non-Christian* sources.

If the New Testament is fictional, one would have to wonder why the writers went to such great lengths to mention real people, during specific times in history, and at real locations.

The above concerns the New Testament. What about the Old Testament?

Scores of items have been verified. Visitors to Israel can walk through Hezekiah's tunnel or see the temple mount—built first by Solomon, rebuilt by Zerubbabel, and then added to by King Herod. Some of the results from the 70 A.D. destruction of Jerusalem remain apparent, such as mounds of stones that were cast down from the temple still positioned where they fell nearly two thousand years ago. Without getting us side-tracked, Jesus predicted this destruction, even declaring that not one stone of the temple would be left in place (Matthew 24:2).

Jerusalem was destroyed four decades after Jesus' death and resurrection. This included the burning of the temple. Historians tell us that the intense heat melted the temple's gold, which ran down between the various stones. To get to these riches, the Romans had to tear down the temple, stone by stone. Not one was left standing—just as Jesus had prophesied four decades earlier. But I digress.

3. **Eyewitness Accounts**

The first four books of the New Testament are referred to as the "Gospels"—the "Good News." The authors were close associates of Jesus or friends of those who were close to Jesus. The Gospel historians Matthew and John were disciples. The Gospel historian Mark was a companion of Peter, a disciple. Luke was a companion of Paul and traveled with him as we see affirmed in both Luke's writings and Paul's writings. Luke not only wrote a historical account of Jesus (the book of Luke), but also wrote of the early church and the acts of the Apostles (the book of Acts, as mentioned above). In addition to his Gospel, we have letters written by the disciple/Apostle John, as well as a vision of end times given to John. We also have letters written by the disciple/Apostle Peter. I focus on these individuals because they either saw the resurrected Jesus or were close associates to those who saw Jesus. For what it's worth (and they will be mentioned below), James and Jude were Jesus' half-brothers. Both ridiculed Jesus until after the crucifixion and resurrection. Both are eyewitnesses and both have writings that have been included as part of the New Testament.

Let's read how the disciple/Apostle John describes his *eyewitness experiences* regarding Jesus:

> That which was from the beginning, which *we have heard*, which *we have seen with our own eyes*, which *we have gazed upon and touched with our own hands*— this is the Word of life. And this is the life that was revealed; *we have seen* it and testified to it, and we proclaim to you the eternal life that was with the Father and was revealed to us.
>
> We proclaim to you *what we have seen and heard*, so that you also may have fellowship with us. And this fellowship of ours is with the Father and with His Son, Jesus Christ. We write these things so that our joy may be complete.

And this is the message *we have heard* from Him and announce to you . . .
(emphasis added). [7]

And note how he attests the veracity of what he shares:

This is the disciple *who testifies* to these things and who has written them down.
And we know that *his testimony is true* (emphasis added).[8]

4. Corroborating Accounts

Many remain unaware of this, but we have numerous writings outside of the Bible, writings from non-Christian sources—including those *hostile* to Christianity—that confirm much of what the Bible tells us.[9] If we pieced together information *just from these writers alone*, again, writers that are not Christian, we would know the following:

1. Jesus lived during the time of Tiberius Caesar.
2. He lived a virtuous life.
3. He performed miracles.
4. He had a brother named James.
5. He was acclaimed to be the Jewish Messiah.
6. He was crucified under Pontius Pilate.
7. He was crucified on the eve of the Jewish Passover.
8. Darkness and an earthquake occurred when Jesus died.

---

[7] This comes from a letter John wrote which is part of the New Testament writings: 1 John 1:1–5.

[8] This comes from the concluding words of the Gospel of John, John 21:24.

[9] See Robert E. Van Voorst, *Jesus Outside the New Testament: An Introduction to the Ancient Evidence* (Grand Rapids: William B. Eerdmans Publishing, 2000). Writings come from Thallos, Pliny the Younger, Suetonius, Tacitus, Mara bar Serapion, Lucian of Samosata, Celsus, and Josesphus. Though dated much later (but based on oral accounts), Jewish rabbinic writings also mention Jesus.

9. His disciples believed he rose from the dead.

10. His disciples were willing to die for their belief.

11. Christianity spread rapidly as far as Rome.

12. His disciples denied the Roman gods and worshipped Jesus as God.

Keep in mind, all of the above can be pieced together from ancient writings *outside of the Bible*, including from sources we would call hostile witnesses.

Let's look at some of these writings in more detail. The Roman historian Josephus (who was a Jew), mentions Jesus on two occasions in his *Jewish Antiquities*. Here is one of the references:

> About this time there lived Jesus, a wise man, if indeed one ought to call him a man. For he ... wrought surprising feats.... He was the Christ. When Pilate ...condemned him to be crucified, those who had . . . come to love him did not give up their affection for him. On the third day he appeared ... restored to life.... And the tribe of Christians ... has ... not disappeared.[10]

This was written by a non-Christian who lived 37 – 100 A.D.

---

[10] Because Josephus' writing mentions Jesus (as well as John the Baptizer), these writings were maintained by early Christians, including copying them for posterity. Scholars do not attribute all of this statement to Josephus and suggest this text was altered, possibly sometime in the third or fourth centuries A.D. But they only point to small sections that might have been altered, such as the phrase "if indeed one ought to call him a man." This is suspect in that it implies that Jesus was more than human, and it is quite unlikely that Josephus would have said this. It is also difficult to believe he would have asserted that Jesus was the Christ, especially when, later in his writing, he refers to Jesus as "the so-called" Christ. Finally, the claim that on the third day Jesus appeared to his disciples restored to life, inasmuch as it affirms Jesus' resurrection, is quite unlikely to have come from a non-Christian. But even if we disregard the questionable parts of this passage, we are still left with a good deal of corroborating information about the biblical Jesus. For a more in-depth treatment of this writing from Josephus, see Van Voorst, *Jesus Outside the New Testament*, 81-104.

The second, though less revealing, reference from Josephus describes the condemnation of one "James" by the Jewish Sanhedrin (James, the half-brother of Jesus was killed in 62 A.D.; the Sanhedrin was equivalent to Judaism's supreme court). James, says Josephus, was "the brother of Jesus the so-called Christ." (Here it is beneficial to remember that the word "Christ" is a title. It is Greek for the Hebrew term we transliterate "Messiah.")

From Josephus, we read that Jesus was a wise man who performed surprising feats. And although he was crucified under Pilate, his disciples were emboldened to follow him and became known as Christians. When we combine these statements with Josephus' later reference to Jesus as "the so-called Christ," a rather detailed picture emerges which harmonizes with the biblical record. The "biblical Jesus" and the "historical Jesus" are one and the same.

Including Josephus there are at least eight known non-Christian writers who mention Jesus within 150 years of his life. This doesn't sound like many, but we should put this into perspective. There are only nine non-Christian writers over this same period who mention Tiberius Caesar—*the emperor or Rome at the time of Jesus!*

If you include Christian sources, authors mentioning Jesus outnumber those mentioning Tiberius 41 to 10! We have more knowledge about Jesus than we do many of the other individuals from this period, with information on Jesus coming from non-biblical, non-Christian sources as we've mentioned.

5. **Consistency**

As mentioned, the Bible is not one book. It is a collection of 66 books written over a period of some 1500 years by 40 different authors. And yet the consistency of the Bible can clearly be seen (for more information on this, I recommend both volumes of *A Forty-Day Study of the Biblical Story*[11]). No other writing or group of writings has this same characteristic.

---

[11] Rick Jory, *A Forty-Day Study of the Biblical Story: The Story of Christ* (Bloomington, WestBow Press, 2020). Volume One covers the Old Testament, Volume Two focuses mainly on the Gospels of the New Testament.

6. **Prophetic Accuracy**

The Bible talks about events in advance of their occurrence—and does so with unbelievable accuracy. One scholar writes, "The very dimension of the sheer fulfillment of prophecy of the Old Testament Scriptures should be enough to convince anyone that we are dealing with a supernatural piece of literature…God has himself planted within the Scriptures an internal consistency that bears witness that this is his Word."[12] There are numerous books available that analyze biblical prophecy and fulfilment. One I'd recommend is *The Popular Encyclopedia of Bible Prophecy* from Harvest House Publishers.

Much has been written about the numerous prophecies which Jesus fulfilled. Volume one of *A Forty-Day Study of the Biblical Story* covers the Old Testament from the perspective of how it centers on Jesus of Nazareth—with these writings being written centuries before his appearance on Earth.[13] But as another starting point, you might read Psalm 22, written a thousand years before Jesus, and Isaiah 53, written seven hundred years before Jesus (we'll look at Isaiah 53 below). Both cover the rejection and crucifixion of Jesus in stunning detail and accuracy despite being written even before execution by crucifixion had come into use.

Matthew's Gospel is also beneficial to read in that he was writing mainly to a Jewish audience, and he spends considerable time pointing out how Jesus of Nazareth fulfilled Jewish prophecy.

While Paul's writing in his letters to the Romans doesn't deal with prophecy, per se, this, along with the book of Hebrews, explains Jesus in the context of God's overall plan of humankind's redemption.

To help us understand prophetic accuracy, let's just look at a sampling of prophecies that come from the prophet Isaiah (this is a partial listing). Jesus claimed to be the Messiah and Son of God, so these prophecies concern Jesus of Nazareth:

---

[12] Unfortunately, I've misplaced the source for this quote.

[13] Rick Jory, *A Forty-Day Study of the Biblical Story: The Story of Christ, Volume One: Preparing the Way* (Bloomington: WestBow Press, 2020).

- His will be a virgin birth (Isaiah 7:14).
- He will be called Immanuel—God with us (Isaiah 7:14).
- He will carry titles such as Wonderful, Counselor, Mighty God, Everlasting Father, Prince of Peace (Isaiah 9:6).
- Nations will seek him (Isaiah 11:10).
- God's Spirit will rest on him (Isaiah 11:2).
- He will judge the nations in righteousness (Isaiah 11:4–5).
- Some of his teachings will fall on deaf ears (Isaiah 6:9–10).
- He will be a stone that causes people to stumble (Isaiah 8:14).
- His ministry will begin in Galilee (Isaiah 9:1–2).
- He will draw the Gentiles to himself (Isaiah 11:10).
- He will have a miraculous ministry (Isaiah 35:5–6).
- He will be preceded by someone coming before him (Isaiah 40:3–4).
- He will possess God's Spirit. He will be a servant. He will be gentle in his ministry and will eventually be ruler over all the earth (Isaiah 42:1–4).
- He will have authority over all judgment (Isaiah 22:22).
- He will conquer death (Isaiah 25:7–8).

Isaiah 52:13 to the end of Isaiah 53 is perhaps the most profound text in all of Isaiah's writing (and perhaps in all of the Bible when it comes to prophecy). Here, the Messiah is described not as conquering and ruling King, but as the Suffering Servant that would be rejected and die for the sins of humankind. Preceding this section, Isaiah foretold that this Servant of God would be spat upon and beaten (Isaiah 50:6). Starting in Isaiah 52:13, we learn additional details. Here is a partial listing:

- He will be despised and rejected (Isaiah 53:3).
- He will be disfigured by suffering (Isaiah 52:14).
- Our sins will be placed upon him (Isaiah 53:6).
- He will die for our sins (Isaiah 53:7–8).

- He will be silent before his accusers and voluntarily accept punishment for our sins (Isaiah 53:7).
- He will be buried in a rich man's tomb and "numbered with the transgressors" (Isaiah 53:9, 12).

This is written by a man that lived 700 years before Jesus of Nazareth was born. And yet it is a remarkable, accurate description of Jesus. It would be convenient for the skeptics to suggest that Isaiah's writing was modified after Jesus was on Earth to match what Jesus experienced. In other words, perhaps the text was altered so that one could readily see Jesus was the person the prophet Isaiah was speaking about.

This option isn't open to us.

First, the Jews who, for the most part, do not believe in Jesus would never want to modify their sacred writings in any way that would suggest the one *they rejected* was the Messiah.

But secondly, as mentioned, the discovery of the Great Isaiah Scroll shows changes to the text have been minimal. As mentioned, this copy of Isaiah's writing is dated to at least one hundred years *before* the birth of Christ—and some scholars suggest it is even older than that. The text of this ancient writing—text that pre-dates Jesus—matches what we have today. The text could not have been changed to match what Jesus went through.

But there's one other possibility. Perhaps Jesus structured his life to match what Isaiah wrote as well as to fulfill the other numerous prophecies concerning the Messiah.

This is an interesting speculation—but let's look at some of this in detail. Isaiah wrote, "he was assigned a grave with the wicked." The word "wicked" is plural. How could Jesus organize his death to occur between thieves (plural)? Isaiah continues, "and with a rich man in His death." "Rich man" is singular. How could Jesus orchestrate his burial to be in a rich man's tomb?

Looking at other items from Isaiah, how could Jesus orchestrate being beaten and spat upon? If we go outside the Isaiah text, how could he assure that he was a descendant in King David's family tree? Or that he was born in Bethlehem? Simply read Psalm 22, written a thousand years before the crucifixion, and notice the remarkable accuracy foretelling the crucifixion of Jesus.

But most importantly, how could Jesus predict that he would rise from the dead? How does one plan all of this and then makes sure it occurs flawlessly?

7. **Expert scrutiny**

The early church had extremely high standards for what books were judged to be authentic and to be included in the Bible. A book had to have been written by an Apostle or someone in his immediate circle. The writing also had to conform to basic Christian faith and had to be in widespread use among the many churches.

Throughout the centuries, these sacred writings have been scrutinized by scholars throughout the world. William Ramsay's archeological exploits to investigate the truthfulness of the book of Acts is one example. Today, Lee Strobel, Gary Habermas, Craig Blomberg and numerous others have investigated, researched, and scrutinized the biblical text and the historicity of the events associated with Jesus.

8. **Leader Acceptance**

The greatest thinkers and philosophers throughout history have affirmed the truth and impact of the Bible. This is true of much of the scientific community of distant past. They recognized that if a rational God made all that there is, all that there is can be subjected to discovery. Nature's laws (natural laws) could be revealed. All of this would point to the mind and attributes of God. The popular author Eric Metaxis writes:

> What a strange reversal of fortune it seems. Far from the idea that science and
> faith are enemies, or that science is increasingly pushing back any need we have
> for God, we discover that the forward march of science is instead pushing back
> the argument against God. The Creator God of the Bible is a God *whose existence
> is increasingly bolstered by science* (emphasis added).[14]

---

[14] Eric Metaxas, *Is Atheism Dead?* (Washington D.C.: Salem, 2021), 38.

9. **Global Influence**

The writings contained in the Bible come from a small geographic region of minor importance to the great kingdoms of the world. And yet, the Bible and its principles have become the foundation for much of the laws and practices found throughout the world. The Bible has affected law, art, music, architecture, and literature. As mentioned above, it has also had a major impact on science. If a rational God created the universe, His laws could be discovered—so thought Isaac Newton, Robert Boyle, Francis Bacon, Johannes Kepler, and others.

10. **Changed Lives**

History has provided numerous examples of individuals whose lives have been dramatically changed through their belief and trust in the God of the Bible. When Jesus was arrested, his disciples scattered and hid. Later they would stand within the Jerusalem temple—the holiest site in all of Judea—and proclaim the resurrection of Jesus. They held on to this claim despite eventual persecution. Later, all but John would be martyred, with each man willing to die for proclaiming Jesus as being the resurrected Lord and Savior.

Another transformed life was that of Rabbi Saul (Hebrew name) who became the Apostle Paul (Paul being his Roman name). He went from imprisoning Jews who believed in Jesus as God's Anointed ("Messiah" or "Christ") to becoming the greatest Christian missionary of the first century.[15]

Augustine (a hedonist); Martin Luther (on his way to becoming a lawyer); John Newton, (a sailor/slave trader and the author of "Amazing Grace"); C. S. Lewis (a reluctant skeptic)—all went

---

[15] "Messiah" comes from the Hebrew term. "Christ" comes from the Greek term. Both mean "anointed."

through profound life changes due to their acceptance of Christ and the words found in the Bible. The list is endless.[16]

We can trust what the Bible has to say.

We've gone through the above because we've used writings from the Bible in our preceeding discussion. And we'll continue looking at information from the Bible as we proceed looking into the death and resurrection of Jesus of Nazareth. But we won't limit our investigation to the Bible only.

---

[16] The dissertation for my second doctorate involved interviewing dozens of once helpless and once hopeless drug addicts—all transformed by the power of Scripture. Many had been incarcerated numerous times. Most had become involved in various crimes committed to get money to support their drug habits. It was only when these men and women were exposed to the Bible that they were able to discontinue substance abuse and begin the process of repairing their lives.

10. THE RELIABILITY OF OUR INFORMATION CONCERNING THE RESURRECTION

Having briefly looked at the Bible and how it is trustworthy, we're ready to look at the resurrection of Jesus of Nazareth. The theologian and author, Timothy Keller, writes, "If Jesus rose from the dead, then you have to accept all that he said; if he didn't rise from the dead, then why worry about any of what he said? The issue on which everything hangs is not whether or not you like his teaching but whether or not he rose from the dead."[17]

Christianity hinges on whether this man, Jesus of Nazareth, did in fact come back from the dead. If Jesus didn't rise from the grave, he was a deceiver and a lunatic. He's not to be trusted—much less followed or revered. If the resurrection did not occur, the Christian worldview is based on falsehoods and should be rejected. As the Apostle Paul wrote, "If Jesus has not been raised, preaching is useless, and our faith is useless" (1 Corinthians 15:14). If the resurrection didn't happen, those of us trusting in Jesus are fools.

So much hinges upon the resurrection that we should ask ourselves, did the resurrection actually occur? Are there sources outside of the Christian community that can affirm this?

And before there can be resurrection, there must be death. Did Jesus actually die on the cross? We must assure ourselves that Jesus truly died on the cross. If he did not die, eyewitnesses that saw him after his

---

[17] Timothy Keller, *The Reason for God: Belief in an Age of Skepticism* (New York: Penguin Books, 2008), 210.

ordeal could have simply been seeing a *resuscitated* Jesus—a man who never really died and hence did not come back from the grave. And if Jesus truly died, then we must find out if he was truly resurrected. Did he truly come back to life?

We are going to answer these questions. We'll rely upon the biblical text. What we have shared previously helps us understand the reliability and accuracy of this text. But we are also going to look at sources outside of the Bible. Some will date back to first century writings, but we'll also look at recent materials, including an article in the secular, peer-reviewed *Journal of the American Medical Association* published in the 1980s.

We'll also rely upon the work of the popular author Lee Strobel. Strobel's background deserves sharing. He was a dyed-in-the-wool atheist. In his words, "My skepticism bubbled over into cynicism and cemented me into my atheism." When his wife became a follower of Jesus and a Christian, he set out to remove her from this cult. Strobel was well equipped for this task. He had a degree in journalism and a law degree from Yale. His occupation was that of being the legal editor for the *Chicago Tribune*. Strobel was schooled in the correct methods of investigation and the value of skepticism.

Strobel thought he could spend a weekend doing a bit of research and convince his wife of her faulty thinking. And he centered this on an attempt to disprove the resurrection. Per Strobel, "Anyone can claim to be the Son of God. But if someone could substantiate that assertion by returning to life after being certifiably dead and buried—well that would be compelling confirmation that he was telling the truth. Even for a skeptic like me."[18] We'll be looking at some of Strobel's findings. We'll also be using material from Richard

---

[18] There are three major sources for the information I attribute to Lee Strobel. One is a presentation I attended several years ago at Cherry Hills Community Church on the outskirts of Denver. The other is the small book titled, *The Case for Easter: A Journalist Investigates Evidence for the Resurrection* (Grand Rapids: Zondervan, 2003). The third is Strobel's message to the congregation of Dallas First Baptist Church on October 24, 2021. It may still be available online via the church's website (www.firstdallas.org). It might also be available via the following link:
https://www.firstdallas.org/media/messages/?date=&sermon_series=&speaker=Lee+Strobel&book=&chapter=&search_term= (accessed November 6, 2021).

Swinburne's *The Resurrection of God Incarnate*.[19] Swinburne is a Fellow of the British Academy and was the Nolloth Professor of the Philosophy of the Christian Religion at Oxford. Materials also came from lectures by Dr. Gary Habermas. Many of his materials are available online.[20]

There are two other references that supplement the material. One is Robert Van Voorst's *Jesus Outside the New Testament*.[21] A second is J. Daniel Hays' *A Christian's Guide to Evidence for the Bible*.[22] My favorite professor for my master's level coursework at Denver Seminary was Dr. Craig Blomberg. He has written several books on the reliability of the New Testament, and these are also of value.[23]

This investigation should follow principles that forensic scientists use to determine the reliability of testimony, asking questions such as:

1. Do we have testimony from the time of the event?
2. Is it eyewitness testimony?
3. Do we have testimony from more than one eyewitness and are these eyewitnesses independent sources?
4. Are the eyewitnesses trustworthy?
5. Do we have corroborating evidence from other sources? For example, is there archeological support?
6. Do we have testimony from individuals who have nothing to gain by offering their testimony?

---

[19] Richard Swinburne, *The Resurrection of God Incarnate* (Oxford: Clarendon Press, 2003).

[20] Dr. Habermas's website is www.garyhabermas.com.

[21] Robert E. Van Voorst, *Jesus Outside the New Testament: An Introduction to the Ancient Evidence* (Grand Rapids: William B. Eerdmans Publishing, 2000).

[22] J. Daniel Hays, *A Christian's Guide to Evidence for the Bible: 101 Proofs from History and Archaeology* (Grand Rapids: Baker Books, 2020).

[23] See, for example, Craig L. Blomberg, *The Historical Reliability of the Gospels* (Downers Grove: IVP Academic, 2007) or Craig L. Blomberg, *The Historical Reliability of the New Testament: Countering the Challenges to Evangelical Christian Beliefs* (Nashville: B&H Academic, 2016).

7. Does the testimony contain events or details that are embarrassing to those providing the testimony? The inclusion of embarrassing details or items that make those testifying appear in an unfavorable light suggest the testimony has not been embellished.

Using these principles and resources, what do we find?

1. Do we have testimony from the time of the event?

The New Testament books were written before 100 A.D.—all within seventy years of Jesus' death. But most were written much earlier than 100 A.D. Most were written before 62 A.D. The writings of Paul and Peter had to have early dates because both were executed in Rome by emperor Nero. Mark's writing had to have an early date because it was used by both Matthew and Luke when they wrote their Gospel accounts.

But why did these men wait two or three decades before documenting what they saw? This is not hard to understand. Jesus predicted his return after leaving this earth, and many of the eyewitnesses thought this would happen in their lifetime. There was no need to write anything down. As they got older, though, they realized the need to record for others what they knew concerning Jesus. This was not just something for posterity. Jesus commanded them to be his witnesses throughout the world and promised they would be empowered by the Holy Spirit to accomplish this task (Acts 1:8). Our New Testament is this apostolic witness.

We need to put this in perspective. Virtually everyone has heard of Alexander the Great. The oldest history we have of him is the *Historiae Alexandri Magni* (Latin for "The Histories of Alexander the Great). It was written by the Roman historian Quintus Curtius Rufus *four hundred years after Alexander's life!* We have no original copies of this—none. The earliest surviving manuscript comes from the ninth century!

So, regarding the resurrection and testimony at the time of the event, we have written testimony from eyewitnesses who witnessed the resurrection and provided written documentation within three decades of what they had witnessed.

2. Do we have testimony from eyewitnesses?

Earlier we read John's affirmation of being an eyewitness (1 John 1:1–5, John 21:24). But he's not alone. Matthew, John, Peter, James, and Jude were all eyewitnesses.

Peter, along with John and his brother James, were considered Jesus' "inner circle." Also as mentioned, Mark was a close companion of Peter (and a companion of Paul as well). Luke was a traveling companion of Paul. James was the half-brother of Jesus, as was Jude.

Paul did not begin as a follower of Jesus and was not an eyewitness to the crucifixion or resurrection. He was present when Stephen, Christianity's first martyr, was stoned to death. Paul went through an astonishing transformation—which he claims came about through an appearance of Jesus. Paul went from zealously trying to stamp out Christianity to being its most ardent advocate. We know that after his "conversion" he met with three of the Apostles—Peter, James, and John—all eyewitnesses of the event.[24]

These multiple eyewitnesses help us answer the next question.

3. Do we have testimony from more than one eyewitness? Is there testimony from multiple, independent eyewitness sources?

We have nine ancient sources inside and outside the Bible attesting to the conviction of the disciples that they had encountered the risen Christ. In addition to the individuals mentioned above, note what Paul says to the believers in Corinth:

---

[24] I use "conversion" quite loosely. Paul did not "convert" to Christianity. Christ fulfills Judaism and Paul is what we'd call a "Messianic Jew"—a believer in Jesus as the Jewish Messiah. Paul was called to this role before birth! (see Galatians 1:15).

For what I received I passed on to you as of first importance: that Christ died for our sins according to the Scriptures, that He was buried, that He was raised on the third day according to the Scriptures, and that He appeared to Cephas [Peter] and then to the Twelve. After that, He appeared to more than five hundred brothers at once, *most of whom are still living*, though some have fallen asleep. Then He appeared to James, then to all the apostles. And last of all He appeared to me also, as to one of untimely birth. (1 Corinthians 15:3–8, emphasis added)

Paul claims Jesus appeared to more than five hundred people after his death and goes on to write, "most of whom are still living." In effect, Paul is saying, "Hey, there are witnesses out there . . . they are still around . . . you can go talk to them if you want."

We should pause and look at this text from Paul in greater detail. He begins, "For what I received I passed on to you as of first importance..." Although the "book" (letter) this comes from is labelled "First Corinthians," we know Paul had written the Christians in Corinth earlier (we do not have this earlier correspondence). We also know that Paul had visited Corinth and that this letter we do have, First Corinthians, was written while Paul was in Ephesus (53 or 54 A.D.). Jesus was crucified in 30 or 33 A.D. (most scholars say 30 A.D.). So, this letter is written twenty or so years after Jesus' death and resurrection. When Paul writes, "For what I received I passed on to you . . ." scholars see in this section of Paul's letter an early Christian creed that Paul learned and passed on to the believers in Corinth. It is a summary of the Gospel:

... that Christ died for our sins according to the Scriptures, that He was buried, that He was raised on the third day according to the Scriptures, and that He appeared to Cephas and then to the Twelve. (1 Corinthians 15:3–5)

We can break this down as follows:

1. Christ died for our sins.

2. This was done according to the Scriptures.

3. He was buried.

4. He was raised on the third day—also according to the Scriptures.

5. He appeared to Peter and then to the Twelve.

Again, scholars suggest this was an early Christian creed, but when, where, and how did Paul get this?[25] We can't be certain, but we know three years after Paul's conversion, he met with three of the Apostles in Jerusalem and he was probably made aware of this at that time.

So, when was Paul's conversion? Scholars suggest Paul's conversion came within 3 years of the crucifixion.

So if Paul received the specifics concerning Jesus' death and resurrection when he met with Apostles in Jerusalem, it must have been only six or seven years after the event. This (along with other items) assures us that resurrection cannot be a myth that developed over time. The assertion of the resurrection began immediately. We also know this from Acts 2 and can deduce this from other sources.

4. Are the eyewitnesses trustworthy?

We'll see below (item 6), part of what makes the testimony of an eyewitness trustworthy is if that person has nothing to gain and much to lose for what they proclaim. In their world of Judaism, what the disciples proclaimed—that Jesus of Nazareth rose from the grave and was the Messiah—meant loss of friends and family and eventual martyrdom. There was nothing to be gained by the assertion they

---

[25] There are a number of technical reasons scholars attribute this as an early creed. Some include: 1) Paul introduces this text with the words, "received" and "passed on" (or "delivered"). These are rabbinic terms indicating the transmission, or passing on, of a holy tradition. 2) The style of the text and its parallelism indicate it's a creed. 3) The original text uses "Cephas" for Peter. Cephas is Aramaic and is used in the earliest of texts. 4) The creed uses phrases not attributed to Paul, such as "the third day," or "the Twelve."

made that Jesus rose from the grave—and much to lose. There is no reason to suggest these were not trustworthy individuals.

5. Do we have corroborating evidence from other sources? For example, in looking at biblical events, is there archeological support?

Most of what we know about the ancient world is based on one or maybe two sources. For the life, death, and resurrection of Jesus, we not only have multiple early accounts, but we also have five ancient sources outside the Bible confirming and corroborating his death.

We've already covered some of the materials that we find outside of the Bible when we looked at writings from Josephus. Robert E. Van Voorst provides translations of writings from the following.[26] These were not eyewitnesses, but they do confirm some of the events concerning Jesus and the early Christians:

- Thallos
- Pliny (the Younger)
- Suetonius
- Tacitus
- Mara bar Serapion
- Lucian of Samosata
- Celsus
- Josephus

Though rare (as would be expected), there are also references in Jewish writings (rabbinic traditions).

---

[26] Robert E. Van Voorst, *Jesus Outside the New Testament: An Introduction to the Ancient Evidence* (Grand Rapids: William Eerdmans Publishing, 2000).

We've looked at Josephus. We know the Jewish Talmud mentions Jesus, as does a man named Pliny and someone named Lucian.[27] We also have the writings of the Roman historian Tacitus, with a passage that historian Edwin Yamauchi labels as being "probably the most important reference to Jesus outside the New Testament."[28] Reporting on Emperor Nero's decision to blame the Christians for the fire that destroyed Rome in 64 A.D., Tacitus writes: "...Nero substituted as culprits and punished in the most unusual way those hated for their shameful acts, called "Chrestians." The founder of this name, Christ, had been executed in the reign of Tiberius by the procurator Pontius Pilatus. Suppressed for a time, the deadly superstition erupted again not only in Judea, the origin of this evil, but also in the city [Rome]."[29]

What can we learn from this ancient, and rather unsympathetic reference to Jesus and the early Christians? Tacitus reports Christians derived their name from a historical person called Christ (Christus in Latin). A more direct translation says this person "suffered the extreme penalty," which would be a reference to the Roman method of execution (crucifixion). This is said to have occurred during the reign of Tiberius and by the sentence of Pontius Pilatus—confirming what the Gospels tell us about the death of Jesus and the role played by Pontius Pilate, the Roman governor.

But what are we to make of Tacitus' rather enigmatic statement, "the deadly superstition" (or in some translations, "a most mischievous superstition") associated with Christ's death? Notice that whatever this superstition was, it arose not only in Judea, but also in Rome.

---

[27] Lucian does not mention Jesus by name but mentions Christians and a "distinguished personage who introduced their novel rites and was crucified on that account." See Lucian, "The Death of Peregrine," 11-13, in *The Works of Lucian of Samosata*, transl. by H. W. Fowler and F. G. Fowler, 4 vols. (Oxford: Clarendon, 1949), vol. 4., cited in Habermas, *The Historical Jesus*, 206.

[28] This material comes from Lee Strobel, *The Case for Christ* (Grand Rapids: Zondervan, 1998).

[29] As translated text, various versions are available with slight modifications. This version comes from Van Voorst, *Jesus Outside the New Testament*, 41-2. "Chrestians" is a misspelling, of course ("Christians"). "Christ" is not a name but a title, which Tacitus did not realize. While The text goes on to describe Nero having captured Christians torn to death by dogs, crucified, or set afire to provide lighting to the emperor's massive garden ("burning torches").

One historian suggests Tacitus is "bearing indirect ... testimony to the conviction of the early church that the Christ who had been crucified had risen from the grave."[30] While this interpretation is admittedly speculative, it does help to explain the otherwise bizarre occurrence of a rapidly growing religion based on the worship of a man who had been crucified as a criminal! Keep in mind, it was less than three hundred years later that Christianity not only became accepted by Rome but was made the official religion of the Roman Empire!

What about archeological support? We know the veracity of the New Testament writers from the numerous archeological discoveries that confirm the accuracy of their writings.[31] But what about the resurrection? Does it have any support from archeology? Archeologists believe we know the place of the crucifixion, as well as the tomb that once contained the body. Of course, no one can point to the earthly remains of Jesus—but this cannot be considered as an argument for resurrection.

As to Roman crucifixion and the practice of nailing victims to wooden crosses, we have archeological evidence of this practice.[32] Perhaps the best-known example was the discovery of a heel bone that still contained the nail from crucifixion (apparently the nail hit a knot in the wood of a cross and became bent and could not be removed from the victim).[33]

---

[30] N.D. Anderson, *Christianity: The Witness of History* (London: Tyndale, 1969), 19, cited in Gary R. Habermas, *The Historical Jesus* (Joplin, Missouri: College Press Publishing Company, 1996), 189-190.

[31] We can deduce some of the historicity concerning Jesus from some of his teachings. In a parable Jesus mentions a vineyard with a wall, a watchtower, and a winepress. Archeologists have uncovered the ruins of a vineyard in Nazareth, the boyhood home of Jesus, that includes a wall, a watchtower, and a winepress. See Matthew 23:33–46.

[32] See, for example, Nicole Arce, "Archeologists Find Rare Remains Of Man Who Died On A Cross" in *Science,* June 6, 2018. Available at. https://www.techtimes.com/articles/229414/20180606/archaeologists-find-rare-remains-of-man-who-died-on-a-cross.htm (accessed November 8, 2021).

[33] See Peter Grose, "Find of Crucified Skeleton Is Linked to a Bent Nail," *The New York Times*, January 4, 1971. Available at. https://www.nytimes.com/1971/01/04/archives/find-of-crucified-skeleton-is-linked-to-a-bent-nail-twisting-of.html (accessed November 8, 2021).

6. Do we have testimony from individuals who have nothing to gain by offering their testimony?

Part of what makes the testimony of an eyewitnesses trustworthy is that they have nothing to gain and much to lose for what they proclaim. The disciples and eyewitnesses abandoned long-held sacred beliefs and practices, and adopted new ones right after what they claim as the resurrection. This happened overnight. Something must have caused this to have occurred. For James and Jude, half-brothers of Jesus, we know they did not become believers until after they had seen the resurrected Jesus.

In their world of Judaism, what the disciples proclaimed—that Jesus of Nazareth rose from the grave and was the Messiah—meant loss of friends and family. They did not deny their testimony under persecution, threat, and eventual death. There was no reason, no incentive, for these eyewitnesses to lie. On the contrary, they could have escaped considerable hardship if they simply denied what they had seen.

7. Does the testimony contain events or details that are embarrassing to those providing the testimony?

If those providing the testimony include embarrassing details, chances are they are being forthright, open, and honest in what they share. As we read the Gospel accounts, we see example after example where the disciples lack faith and don't place their trust in Jesus. They depict themselves as cowards and as being ignorant regarding many of the things Jesus was saying at the time these were spoken.

But the writers and eyewitnesses also do not hold back in including embarrassing details about Jesus. They record his own mother and brothers calling him "out of his mind" (Mark 3:21). They write of Jesus allowing his feet to be wiped by a prostitute (Luke 7:36–39). They don't leave out examples where people called him a drunkard, madman and demon possessed (for example, Matthew 11:19; John 10:20; Mark 3:22).

There are numerous other details that suggest what we read is not made up or embellished:
- Why would the writers have Jesus buried in the tomb of a member of the Sanhedrin?
- Why would another member of the Sanhedrin bring the necessary agents to prepare the body of Jesus for burial? Surely, they would have chosen the disciples to do this—unless the stories

regarding Joseph of Arimathea and Nicodemus were actually true and the writers were recording what actually happened (we'll look at this).

- Why would the empty tomb have been found by women? The testimony from women carried no weight in this culture.
- Why would we read that many Jewish priests became believers (Acts 6:7)?
- Why would the New Testament writers challenge their readers to check their stories (see for example 2 Corinthians 12:12 and 1 Corinthians 15:1–7)?

One would question the inclusion of these items if the biblical record were not historically accurate and true.

We have no reason to question the veracity and accuracy of the events described by the New Testament authors. We know all but John of the original disciples, as well as the Apostle Paul went to their deaths rather than recant their stories.

We're now ready to return to our main questions:

- Did Jesus really die? In order to authenticate the resurrection, we must be secure in knowing Jesus did in fact die on the cross and was not "faking it."
- Did the resurrection truly happen?

We'll now answer these. Though not central to this discussion, per se, we find some interesting information concerning the tomb of Jesus being found empty. We'll add this to our discussion as well.

11. Did Jesus Really Die?

A medical doctor and team from the Mayo Clinic's Department of Pathology researched the death of Jesus of Nazareth analyzing the available evidence (written accounts) using current medical science. These results were published in the prestigious *Journal of the American Medical Association*—a scientific, peer-reviewed medical journal. The article concludes, "Clearly the weight of the historical and medical evidence indicates that Jesus was dead [even] before the wound to his side was inflicted." This comes from the March 21, 1986, JAMA article titled, "On the Physical Death of Jesus Christ."[34]

But we do not have to rely upon this to assert that Jesus really died. If we examine what we know about the hours leading up to and including the crucifixion, as well as what happened immediately after the crucifixion, we should be able to come to our own conclusion. To this we can add what we know about Roman punishment, which could include both flogging and crucifixion, and whether someone could survive what Jesus went through.

1. Jesus was in a weakened state. During his prayers in the garden of Gethsemane, he was experiencing intense anxiety. Luke was a physician and describes Jesus' sweat as being like drops of blood falling

---

34 Available at https://jamanetwork.com/journals/jama/article-abstract/403315 (accessed November 6, 2021). Access to the full article requires subscription.

to the ground (Luke 22:44). Perhaps this was hyperbole on Luke's part. But today, medical science is aware of something called hematohidrosis. This is where blood does migrate through the sweat glands when a person is under acute anxiety and stress.

2. After being awake all night, Jesus was placed in a cell at Caiaphas's house. When he is taken to appear before the Roman governor, Pilate is hesitant to execute Jesus. He has Jesus severely beaten, perhaps to appease the crowd that had gathered so they would be satisfied and not demand Jesus' crucifixion. Concerning this beating, the following is an excerpt from *A Forty-Day Study of John's Gospel*:[35]

> Roman flogging was almost as painful as Roman crucifixion. It was so severe that women, Roman senators, and soldiers were exempt from this punishment (soldiers could be flogged due to desertion). To flog or scourge someone was to whip them to the point of death. Historians tell us, six out of ten times the flogging alone was lethal. Those that survived were usually carried away on a stretcher.

> Flogging was carried out using whips made with several single or braided leather thongs of variable lengths. Pieces of metal, small iron balls, or sharp pieces of bone were tied to these at intervals. These would tear into and grab the flesh and tissue of the victim. The victim's bones would sometimes be exposed as the sharp objects on the whips would grab into the tissue and pull it apart. There was massive pain and blood loss.

> Under Jewish law, no one could receive more than forty lashes (Deuteronomy 25:3). In order not to accidentally violate this, the Jews would only give the

---

[35] Rick Jory, *A Forty-Day Study of John's Gospel: Who exactly is Jesus?* (Bloomington: WestBow Press, 2021).

criminal thirty-nine lashes. The apostle Paul was flogged (scourged) five times and refers to this as "forty lashes minus one" (2 Corinthians 11:24). But Jesus' punishment comes from the Romans, not the Jews. The Bible does not tell us how many lashings he received—but there is no reason to assume it was limited to thirty-nine.[36]

3. Blood loss associated with this beating would have most likely led to hypovolemic shock. We have indications that this did occur in that eyewitnesses say Jesus did not have enough strength to carry the cross and fell under its weight. A Roman soldier had to force a bystander, Simon from an ancient Greek colony called Cyrene, to carry the cross.

4. At the crucifixion site, Jesus would have been laid upon the cross to facilitate the nailing of his feet and wrists. These nails were seven to nine inches long. As mentioned earlier, archeologists have recovered the remains of a crucifixion victim with a metal nail still stuck in the bones of this man's heel (a picture of this artifact can be seen by Googling "picture of nail in heel bone from crucifixion" or words similar).

5. Upon being lifted from the ground, the weight of his body, coupled with his arms being outstretched, would mean both shoulders would have become dislocated (this comes from an interview between Strobel and Dr. Alexander Metherell, who holds both a medical degree and a PhD in engineering— see the quote in the next bullet point).

6. Death actually occurs through asphyxiation:

---

[36] Ibid., 460.

Crucifixion is essentially an agonizingly slow death by asphyxiation. The reason is that the stresses on the muscles and diaphragm put the chest into the inhaled position; basically, in order to exhale, the individual must push up on his feet so the tension on the muscles would be eased for a moment. In doing so, the nail would tear through the foot, eventually locking up against the tarsal bones. After managing to exhale, the person would then be able to relax down and take another breath in. Again he'd have to push himself up to exhale, scraping his bloodied back against the coarse wood of the cross. This would go on until complete exhaustion would take over, and the person wouldn't be able to push up and breathe anymore.[37]

7. When it appeared that Jesus had succumbed to death, a Roman soldier thrust a spear into Jesus' side. The disciple John, an eyewitness of these events, records something unexpected. He describes water and blood flowing from this wound (John 19:34). John would have no reason to expect this, nor would he have understood the medical implications of what he was seeing. Since what he saw was unexpected, he recorded it. Today we know what John witnessed is associated with respiratory acidosis. This would occur as Jesus' breathing began to slow down. This is also evidence of both pericardial effusion and pleural effusion. This suggests the Roman spear went through the right lung of Jesus and into his heart. John would be unaware of these implications, of course. He just saw something unusual that left a vivid image, and he writes what he saw.

8. Jesus body was removed from the cross and was prepared for burial per Jewish custom. We are told the body was wrapped in linen clothes and covered with a mixture of myrrh and aloes weighing about seventy-five pounds.

There is no reason to believe Jesus did not die on the cross.

---

[37] Lee Strobel, *The Case for Easter: A Journalist Investigates Evidence for the Resurrection* (Grand Rapids: Zondervan, 2003), 20.

12. WAS THE TOMB OF JESUS REALLY EMPTY?

Though not central to our discussion, if Jesus was seen walking around after his death, we would expect the tomb in which he was laid to be empty. Was it?

Before we get to this, while doing his research on the resurrection, Strobel was made aware that most criminals were not buried after Roman crucifixion. Usually, their corpses remained for birds and various predators to go after.

But the eyewitnesses say Jesus' body was handed over to a man named Joseph of Arimathea. The Bible tells us that Joseph was a member of the Sanhedrin, the supreme court of Judaism. But it was the Sanhedrin who condemned Jesus, with members taking him to Pilate to be executed. Why would Joseph ask for the body so that he could provide a burial? This seems farfetched.

The Gospel writer Luke provides a clue:

Now there was a Council member named Joseph, a good and righteous man, *who had not consented to their decision or action.* (Luke 23:50–51; emphasis added)

Joseph disagreed with the Sanhedrin's decision to hand Jesus over to the Romans for execution. Matthew, an eyewitness and disciple of Jesus, adds to what we know:

When it was evening, there came a rich man from Arimathea named Joseph, *who himself was a disciple of Jesus.* (Matthew 27:57; emphasis added)

While Joseph was a member of the Sanhedrin, he was also a follower of Jesus. It sounds farfetched that such a prominent person would become a follower, but we know Nicodemus, also a member of the Sanhedrin sought out Jesus, and a "large number" of Jewish priests became believers after the resurrection (Acts 6:7).

John, also an eyewitness and disciple, adds to this by telling us that Joseph had to keep his allegiance to Jesus' secret:

Afterward, Joseph of Arimathea, who was a disciple of Jesus (but secretly for fear of the Jews), asked Pilate to let him remove the body of Jesus. Pilate gave him permission, so he came and removed His body. (John 19:38)

We can understand why Joseph wanted the body of Jesus to receive a proper burial. But now we can ask another question. Was Joseph of Arimathea a real person? Couldn't these writers simply make all of this up?

There are documents from history that mention a rich man named Joseph who was in Jerusalem at the time of Jesus. We cannot be certain this is the same Joseph ("Joseph" was the second most common male name among Palestinian Jews).[38] However, there is also a tomb located near the traditional site of Jesus' tomb that is recognized as the tomb of Joseph of Arimathea. In addition, Matthew, Mark, Luke, and John all attest to this man, Joseph of Arimathea, and his role in the burial of Jesus. We have no reason to doubt that Joseph of Arimathea was a man living at the time of Jesus and that he provided the tomb for the body of Jesus.

Let's return to our question. Was the tomb empty?

We know the tomb was sealed and was placed under guard. And while there is much that could be said to prove that the tomb was found to be empty, there is one overriding fact that affirms an empty tomb.

---

[38] See "9 Reasons Why Joseph of Arimathea Was a Real Historical Figure," from *CapturingChristianity* and available at https://capturingchristianity.com/9-reasons-why-joseph-of-arimathea-was-a-real-historical-figure/ (accessed November 8, 2021).

Even the enemies of Jesus admitted the tomb was empty! They claimed Jesus' disciples stole the body. They had no reason to suggest this unless they recognized the body was not in the tomb—that is, they knew the tomb was empty and they had to come up with reasons for this. The tomb being empty had to be explained.

Whether it be the enemies of Jesus, or the followers of Jesus, everybody either implicitly or explicitly concedes the tomb was empty.

And no one has been able to produce a body, of course.

So, we're left with the real issue. Everything centers on *how the tomb became empty.* And this leads to the most important question to address: Did Jesus really rise from the grave?

Those rejecting the resurrection offer several suggestions:

- The Romans took the body.

  This is nonsensical. The Romans wanted Jesus dead. And when people began declaring that Jesus had been resurrected, they could have simply put Jesus' body on display if they were the ones who took it.

- The Jewish authorities took the body.

  This, too, is nonsensical. The Jewish authorities wanted to rid themselves of Jesus. They not only wanted Jesus dead, but they also wanted him to stay dead! They wanted nothing that would draw attention to Jesus.

- The disciples took the body.

  The disciples didn't have the motive, the means, or the opportunity to take the body. And why would they do this? We have seven ancient sources, six of them outside the Bible, that confirm the disciples lived lives of suffering and depravation as a result of their insistence that Jesus rose from the dead. What did the disciples have to gain by taking the body and making up a story—especially since their belief in the resurrection led to their eventual martyrdom?

No, their claims of resurrection were made simply because these claims were true! They talked with the resurrected Jesus. They ate with the resurrected Jesus. They were given instructions by the resurrected Jesus. They knew the truth. And they were willing to proclaim the truth despite rejection, on-going persecution, and eventual martyrdom.

The tomb of Jesus was empty.

13. Did Jesus Rise from the Dead?

We are left with the possibility that Jesus did exactly what he said he would do, which means Jesus is exactly who he says he is. We have nine sources inside and outside the Bible attesting to the conviction of the disciples that they had encountered the risen Christ. In the biblical record, Jesus appears alive in over a dozen different instances to more than five hundred and fifteen people—men, women, daytime appearances, nighttime appearances, appearances to individuals as well as appearances to groups of individuals. The individuals who saw the resurrected Christ include:

- Mary Magdalene (John 20:10–18).
- The other women mentioned by the disciple Matthew (Matthew 28:8–10).
- Cleopas and a second disciple on the road to Emmaus (Luke 24:13–32).
- The eleven disciples and others (Luke 24:33–49).
- Ten of the disciples with Thomas absent (John 20:19–23).
- The disciples along with Thomas (John 20:26–30).
- Seven of the disciples in Galilee (John 21:1–14).
- The disciples once again (Matthew 28:15–20).
- The final appearance to the disciples, now Apostles, before the ascension (Luke 24:50–52; Acts 1:4–9).

We have the creed of 1 Corinthians 15 that affirms the resurrection and mentions eyewitnesses by name. We have Paul's testimony in that he uses this creed, which he probably received when he met with Peter, James, and John when he visited Jerusalem. We have Peter's sermon that is recorded in the book of Acts. We have the accounts from Matthew, Mark, Luke, and John—including the accounts in the book of Acts (see, in particular, the wording found in Acts 2:32; 3:15; 10:41—all representing the words of the Apostle Peter; and Acts 13:31, representing the words of the Apostle Paul). The four Gospels record nine separate appearances of Jesus. Outside the biblical text, we have a letter written to the Corinthians by a Christian named Clement, a church leader ordained by Peter, where he refers to the resurrected Christ. Polycarp, appointed by John to be the bishop of Smyrna, mentions the resurrection of Jesus five times.

In writing to the believers in Corinth, Paul explains: "If Christ has not been raised, our preaching is worthless, and so is your faith" (1 Corinthians 15:14). And that's absolutely correct. But Jesus of Nazareth *was* raised from the dead. The resurrection means we have no reasons to doubt the words and works of Jesus. This single event in history authenticates God's plan to redeem those called into His kingdom.

14. THE RESURRECTION OF JESUS: OUR LORD, SAVIOR, GOD AND KING

The death of Jesus was the ultimate purpose of his ministry. And the resurrection is God's affirmation of this ministry.

Jesus came to defeat death. He came to offer humanity forgiveness.

The Bible teaches that all descendants of Adam have an inherited sin nature and consequently all face death. Physical death is separation from the body. Spiritual death is separation from God. Jesus led a sinless life, but he took upon himself the sins of the world. A righteous God must punish sin, and Jesus accepted God's punishment for our sin. This required the blood of Christ, and the Bible has much to say about this:

- We are cleansed by the blood of Christ:

  … the blood of Jesus His Son cleanses us from all sin. (1 John 1:7)

- The blood of Christ frees us from the bondage of sin:

  Jesus Christ . . . To Him who loves us and has released us from our sins by His blood. (Revelation 1:5)

- Our redemption and forgiveness come through the blood of Christ:

  In Him we have redemption through His blood, the forgiveness of our trespasses, according to the riches of His grace. (Ephesians 1:7)

- The blood of Christ is the payment for our redemption:

  For you know that it was not with perishable things such as silver or gold that you were redeemed from the empty way of life you inherited from your forefathers, but with the precious blood of Christ, a lamb without blemish or spot. (1 Peter 1:18–19)

- We receive sanctification through the blood of Christ:

  And so Jesus also suffered outside the city gate, to sanctify the people by His own blood. (Hebrews 13:12)

- It is the blood of Christ that allows us access to God:

  Therefore, brothers, since we have confidence to enter the Most Holy Place by the blood of Jesus... (Hebrews 10:19)

- The blood of Christ purchased the Church:

  Keep watch over yourselves and the entire flock of which the Holy Spirit has made you overseers. Be shepherds of the church of God, which He purchased with His own blood. (Acts 20:28)

- The reconciliation of all things and the peace we can now possess come through the blood of Christ:

  For God was pleased to have all His fullness dwell in Him, and through Him to reconcile to Himself all things, whether things on earth or things in heaven, by making peace through the blood of His cross. (Colossians 1:19– 20)

- The blood of Christ allows us to be justified—pronounced "not guilty" by God—and to be saved from God's wrath:

  …since we have now been justified by His blood, how much more shall we be saved from wrath through Him! (Romans 5:9)

- It is the blood of Christ that can cleanse our consciences so that we may serve God:

  How much more will the blood of Christ, who through the eternal Spirit offered Himself unblemished to God, purify our consciences from works of death, so that we may serve the living God! (Hebrews 9:14)

Specific to those called into the family of God, we have peace with God (Romans 5:1), there is no condemnation (Romans 8:1), we have been adopted into God's family (Romans 8:14), nothing, nothing whatsoever can separate us from God's love (Romans 8:38, 39)—all because of the blood of Christ.

And through the ordinance of Communion, we are to remember the blood of Christ. At the Last Supper, Jesus took bread and broke it—symbolizing his body broken for us. He then took the cup of wine and told his disciples,

"This cup is the new covenant in My blood, which is poured out for you." (Luke 22:20)

It is the blood of Christ that would be poured out for Jesus' followers. And it is the blood of Christ that ushers in the New Covenant. To understand salvation, it is beneficial to gain an understanding of what this New Covenant is.

The Old Testament describes God's relationship with His chosen people—the people of Israel. A covenant (promise) was made between God and Moses, but this was conditional and temporary. It has been replaced with the New Covenant inagurated by the blood of Christ.

Moses anticipated this. He looked forward to a future time when the people would be given "a mind to understand, eyes to see, or ears to hear" (Deuteronomy 29:4).

Moses foresaw restoration, a time when "The LORD your God will circumcise your hearts and the hearts of your descendants, and you will love Him with all your heart and all your soul, so that you may live" (Deuteronomy 30:6).

The prophet Jeremiah also predicted this new covenant between God and His people:

"Behold, the days are coming," declares the LORD,

when I will make a new covenant

with the house of Israel

and with the house of Judah.

It will not be like the covenant

I made with their fathers

when I took them by the hand

to lead them out of Egypt—

a covenant they broke,

though I was a husband to them,"

declares the LORD.

"But this is the covenant I will make with the house of Israel

after those days, declares the LORD.

I will put My law in their minds

and inscribe it on their hearts.

And I will be their God,

and they will be My people." (Jeremiah 31:31–33)

God also proclaims this through the prophet Ezekiel:

"I will give you a new heart and put a new spirit within you; I will remove your heart of stone and give you a heart of flesh. And I will put My Spirit within you and cause you to walk in My statutes and to carefully observe My ordinances." (Ezekiel 36:26–27)

The prophets foretell of God forming a new promise with His people. It will involve not a changed heart but a new heart. And it will be a covenant where God's Spirit will indwell His people. The law given to Moses and the blood of goats and bulls could not do any of this. It would take the blood of Christ.

The Apostle Paul, like us, lived under the New Covenant. He writes,

…sin shall not be your master, because you are not under law, but under grace." (Romans 6:14)

Because we live under the New Covenant, the law given to Moses is no longer in effect. God's people are under grace. The Old Covenant has been replaced by "a better covenant" (Hebrews 7:22).

Being based on the law, the Old Covenant brought blessings for obedience and punishment—and even death—for disobedience. It required that Israel perform ongoing sacrifices to atone for sin—what we discussed earlier.

Jesus came and fulfilled the law (Matthew 5:17). The New Covenant is based on grace. Christ, the Most Righteous, died for you and me—the unrighteous. The Holy Spirit now brings life to those spiritually dead. And it is because of this that the New Covenant can impart righteousness as well as provide the empowerment that enables its demands to be kept.

And so, at the Last Supper, we hear Jesus say, "This cup is the new covenant in My blood, which is poured out for you." (Luke 22:20)

The blood of Christ has brought us God's new covenant with humanity. It has brought us cleansing, freedom from the bondage to sin, redemption, forgiveness, sanctification, access to God, adoption, security, reconciliation, peace, and justification.

Those who are spiritually awakened and place their faith (trust) in Jesus are justified (considered "not guilty"). We refer to this as salvation—and it is nothing that we do. It is the work of the Father, who calls us into His family, the Son, who died on the cross for the forgiveness of our sins, and the Holy Spirit, who brings us from spiritual death—separation from God, to spiritual life—new life in Christ.

We are not saved by our faith in Christ. We are saved by the blood of Christ—Christ's sacrificial death on the cross.

Had there been no resurrection, there could be no assurance that Jesus truly is the Lamb of God that takes away sin. The resurrection affirms that Jesus is who he claimed to be.

If Jesus of Nazareth had remained in the grave, there would be no salvation.

But he did not remain in the grave.

We can be absolutely certain of the resurrection of Jesus of Nazareth.

BIBLIOGRAPHY

Anderson, N. D. *Christianity: The Witness of History*. London: Tyndale, 1969.

Arce, Nicole. "Archeologists Find Rare Remains Of Man Who Died On A Cross" in *Science,* June 6, 2018. Available at https://www.techtimes.com/articles/229414/ (accessed November 8, 2021).

Blomberg, Craig L. *The Historical Reliability of the Gospels*. Downers Grove: IVP Academic, 2007.

_____. *The Historical Reliability of the New Testament: Countering the Challenges to Evangelical Christian Beliefs*. Nashville: B&H Academic, 2016.

Grose, Peter. "Find of Crucified Skeleton Is Linked to a Bent Nail," *The New York Times*, January 4, 1971. Available at https://www.nytimes.com/1971/01/04/archives/find-of-crucified-skeleton-is-linked-to-a-bent-nail-twisting-of.html (accessed November 8, 2021).

Habermas, Gary R. *The Historical Jesus*. Joplin: College Press Publishing Company, 1996

Hays, J. Daniel. *A Christian's Guide to Evidence for the Bible: 101 Proofs from History and Archaeology*. Grand Rapids: Baker Books, 2020.

Helmenstine, Anne Marie, "How much are the elements in your body worth?" published in *ThoughtCo,*

January 13, 2020 and available at https://www.thoughtco.com/worth-of-your-elements-3976054 (accessed November 23, 2021).

Jory, Rick. *A Forty-Day Study of the Biblical Story: The Story of Christ, Volume One: Preparing the Way.* Bloomington, Westbow Press, 2020.

_____. *A Forty-Day Study of the Biblical Story: The Story of Christ, Volume Two: The Arrival of the Christ.* Bloomington, WestBow Press, 2020.

_____. *A Forty-Day Study of John's Gospel: Who Exactly is Jesus?* Bloomington: WestBow Press, 2021.

"9 Reasons Why Joseph of Arimathea Was a Real Historical Figure." *CapturingChristianity.* Available at https://capturingchristianity.com/9-reasons-why-joseph-of-arimathea-was-a-real-historical-figure/ (accessed November 8, 2021).

Keller, Timothy. *The Reason for God: Belief in an Age of Skepticism.* New York: Penguin Books, 2008.

Metaxas, Eric. *Is Atheism Dead?* Washington D.C.: Salem, 2021.

"On the Physical Death of Jesus Christ" *Journal of the American Medical Association*, March 21, 1986. Available at https://jamanetwork.com/journals/jama/article-abstract/403315 (accessed November 6, 2021).

Strobel, Lee. *The Case for Christ: A Journalist's Personal Investigation of the Evidence for Jesus.* Grand Rapids: Zondervan, 2016.

_____. *The Case for Easter: A Journalist Investigates Evidence for the Resurrection.* Grand Rapids: Zondervan, 2003.

Swinburne, Richard. *The Resurrection of God Incarnate.* Oxford: Clarendon Press, 2003.

Van Voorst, Robert E. *Jesus Outside the New Testament: An Introduction to the Ancient Evidence.* Grand Rapids: William B. Eerdmans Publishing, 2000.

Printed in the United States
by Baker & Taylor Publisher Services